Hunter Johnson Presents...

Old Soul

DEDICATION

This book is dedicated to the prices paid, yesterday, as an investment in tomorrow.

CONTENTS

What God Loves:
Truth

Something to Talk About

My mother—from her seemingly endless wealth of wisdom,
Used to sit me down, when I was young—feeling down and out.
She said, "Baby, don't you worry about them talking;
You just give them something to talk about."

Even if they don't speak on it,
You know that they are watching.
So don't you ever slow down in doing;
And you better not ever think of stopping.

Don't you let whatever they may say,
Make you ever choose to ease up.
They are going to talk, regardless;
Just look at the way that they did Jesus.

If they would drag and scandalize,
And even choose to murder the Messiah,
You think that they would hesitate, at all
With you—trying to make you out to be a liar?

They'll be slow to heap on heaps of praise,
But will run with stories of your tears—
Slow to speak with congratulations,
But quick to run with forked tongues to itching ears.

You cannot afford to wait or delay—
Thinking time is on your side.
No matter what they say to try and dull your shine,
Baby, you have got to stay on your grind.

You may not hit a homerun,
Each time you approach the plate.
But you better stay swinging for the fences,
And do best to pound it over the gate.

Don't you give any of your attention,
To how they try to put you down.
Don't ever settle with scratching the surface—
You make sure that you run it in the ground.

Folks will always be folks,
Making noise and finding a reason to shout.
So do not worry about them not talking;
Just be sure to give them something to talk about.

Coup de Grace

Let's take a stroll down memory lane;
What we are likely to see throughout history,
Is how within the defined confines of war,
Merciful warriors helped the fallen and dying out of their misery.

While hope in things that are to come,
Are not just as life but are of the living—
Just like we can breathe life into them,
We, too, can help to kill them.

Any true friend—be he layman or kin—
Has from two options he must decide.
Though he may not have to push them to grow,
He does not have to help you to make sure that they die.

(Decide...)

The choice is yours, and yours, alone;
You have to deal with it as you go forth.
But I suggest that you choose best—
Value a village that will help to maximize your worth.

Life's landscape is littered with plenty,
Of possibilities of things that could be.
But many dreams were dead on arrival,
From people who had no one to show them what they couldn't see.

It's cool to be liked,
But get around those who want to get you to destiny.
I would rather be an outcast to the coolest in class,
If it meant being somebody to those who see the best in me.

If my dreams MUST die, I'll run on my sword—
At least I would have decided their fate.
But one thing of which I will be damned,
Is lugging around anybody's dead weight.

Analysis Paralysis

Planning is proactive;
It lessens chance of unwanted surprise.
Don't listen if naysayers tell you,
Not to cross your T's and dot your I's.

A little attention to detail
May just prove to be what you need.
To set the stage to obtain success,
Before you decide to proceed.

But when it becomes a problem
And may even bring you sorrow,
Is when thinking of what may come
Begins to plague your mind and makes you fearful of tomorrow

If you are frozen in your tracks
By doing too much analysis,
And it becomes an obsession to plan,
It's unhealthy to growth and is paralysis.

Think of times when you have planned,
And it seemed you took steps back.
Because concentrating on the right move,
In turn, made you too scared to act.

The proposal was seemingly perfect;
There was no doubt that you would get it.
But your second-guessing became a barrier,
And you hesitated and didn't even submit it.

The Tragic Hero

His disposition is so affable;
So focused, he is unflappable.
Though he seems all but magical,
A fatal flaw could make him laughable.

He is a homer; always head to the fence, when he is at bat.
Life's obstacles can't seem to bend him, he is an acrobat.
Fashionable chic fits his physique—
A superhero anyone would marvel at.

He has the smarts characteristic of a doctor—
With the people, a servant king.
Face like you would have seen on a tv screen;
A smile that could grace covers of magazines.

No challenges met, he always exceeds—
Warrior's blood pumps with each breath he breathes.
Mediocrity, to him, is a feared disease.
Through the eyes of vision, he always sees.

Phenom—he is extra special, too.
His life is a walking spectacle.
But where we get it wrong, each time,
Is that we put him on a pedestal.

If he reads his own press, his ascending climb,
Through pride, could become a crawl.
What we need to keep in mind when we see him,
Is that we all possess a fatal flaw.

Who You Fooling?

I am a constant joker;
All day, I laugh and play.
But just know that I understand more than I acknowledge—
I see more than I say.

Don't assume that you are fooling me,
By who it is that you're presumed to be.
I may play into what you present,
But don't believe that you are zoomin' me.

Like anyone, there are two sides—
What actually is and what you let us see.
I analyze and compartmentalize between the show,
And, then, the lies that lie beneath.

You want to say that you're an open book,
And you live your life, transparently.
I am sure that it comes from, largely in part,
Many people just roll with it, apparently.

This is no shade and is not intentioned,
To cause anyone any shame or grief.
I just thought that I would politely ask,
For you to remain true to who you claim to be

The I's Have It

Self is a potent player
And should be esteemed in this.
But recognizing the strength of 'Us'
Is what helps to add the value in this.

Stop thinking of only 'I' and 'Me;'
Yes, we'll always see our prospective, first.
But the value of the collective whole,
Is made greater when see each other's worth.

If we make every chance to take
All that we can for us and ours,
We negate the positive of plurality
And we forfeit the group and it's possible power.

Ascension of our lineage
Is what will probably prove as true.
But if the village stood for cooperative profit,
What would be impossible for us to do?

To once again stand tall with pride
For the good and sake of the tribe,
We may go from trying to survive
And learn what it's like to strive like family and thrive.

So let's change our way of thinking,
And stop crabbing for the jive band.
Doing as Mufasa taught Simba,
Showing him to try and strengthen the Pride Lands.

No more selfishness to be taken forward—
No hurdles that are new to the
Goals of growth and new ways
To add more unity in the community.

Fallacy of Malice

Lately, some of the looks I get,
Make me scratch my head trying to comprehend it.
They look with discontent as if,
Somehow, they have been offended.

If there is something underlying,
I hope they know that it was not intended.
My prayer is that my character's such,
That I will not have to contend it.

Though I know that you can't please everyone,
Or of them, make them a friend.
If there is some wrong I have done,
I would like to make amends.

First, to free myself of sin—
Integrity is the measure of great men.
Then, I hope that they'll deflate the hate,
So that they may be made whole, again.

After I have looked them straight in the face,
To learn the source of their dismay.
And sought to see what was the cause,
That made them turn away.

What else can I do,
In order to attempt to get their forgiveness—
If they have made up in their mind,
That they will never give so I may get it?

What I have come to know for sure,
Is, at that point, it is not my business.
They may just have a problem,
And there is an issue within their spirit.

If they have a fallacy of malice,
And choose to let hate rule them,
They may just be a tool of the devil—
Too, choosing to let the enemy use them.

Ivory Tower

Though I was insistent,
You were resistant.
You could have helped,
To change my life in just an instant.

Despite the fact I was best fit for it,
You dangled it like a carrot.
Pettiness and lust for power,
Made you ensure that I would not have it.

How can you ever hope to see,
The strain of the boots on the ground?
When your ivory tower's so comfy,
You have no need in looking down?

Pedestal can become your pedigree;
Everyday struggles become your jokes.
When you are too far removed,
From what is common to common folk.

You take for granted insurance—
How premiums will be paid.
Overlooking that for some,
Between gas and groceries, a decision must be made.

Your money's long, and the time's long gone—
If you even knew hardship, ever.
What about a little compassion,
For those who have known about surplus, never?

I will follow the wisdom of Psalms,
When it advises and insists that we.
Fret not because of evildoers—
Neither be envious of the workers of iniquity.

In spite of your lapse in judgment,
I won't be the one to judge.
For your malicious misstep,
I won't be the one to hold a grudge.

You've done your best to pick and prod—
And, too, to provide provocation.
As you do, just remember that sin,
Doesn't have to be repaid in one generation.

The psalmist said that there is no begging bread,
For seeds of the righteous; that's explicit.
There are also warnings,
Against the actions of the wicked.

Millie the Manipulator

I never wanted to empower tyrants
Or what's worse never wanted to be,
The one who said and made you question
Where you would be if it had not been for me.

Some will follow this common approach;
They use your need for them to shape and mold you.
Whether money or other things they provide,
They take every chance to manipulate and control you.

They'll freely give you gifts and such—
Even offer to pay the bill of your phone.
The ever-present objective is to have you think,
That you'll never get something as good if gotten on your own.

Molly is one of these;
She can seem to be so kind.
But she proves her true intent;
True colors shine through, time after time.

She'll step in to help you to get to what you lack;
Her slipped dollars help to keep you afloat.
She makes it seem as though she's your biggest supporter,
Saying the right words and peddling hope.

Things that she has in abundance,
She leverages to you, and the trap is set.
You find yourself in a web she weaved;
Now, she has lured you into her debt.

She says, "Pay me when you get it;
There's no rush—repay me when you can."
She knows as long as she holds your debt,
She holds you within her hand.

You believe in and thank her for her benevolence;
You think it's good as long as you pay her back.
What was in the small print of the agreement
Was that her assistance comes with strings attached.

She expects unyielding loyalty;
She makes herself be the only friend you see.
Unwilling to not wield her authority,
She even expects you to hate her enemies.

Any malice that keeps her off balance—
Any hatred satiated in her—
Is enough to stand as proof,
That the borrower becomes slave to the lender.

If I could offer you any advice,
I would try and keep it basic.
Know exactly what's expected in return,
For any help before you decide to take it.

Love, This Day

I long for the day that this is not a thing;
It happens, often, sadly.
We tend to not appreciate what we had,
Until we no longer have it.

We mourn and shake and pull and grab,
Crying through tears that will not desist.
All that comes from what you should've did and would've did,
When you could've did, exists as guilt.

No matter how much grabbing at the casket,
Or how many unspoken words you find you have.
Nothing in this world can be done;
Nothing will bring your loved one back.

That's why, with whatever time you have,
Instead of taking away from their life with strife,
We need to constantly be looking for ways to love,
And trying best to treat each other right.

(Trust me...)

When you give them all you have,
And you choose to leave no doubt,
There will be no need for extended grieving—
No "what if" left to figure out.

Love on your folks while you've got them,
No matter how much they frustrate or aggravate you.
Because regardless of who leaves first,
One day, death will be there to separate you.

When that day comes,
You can visit the cemetery as much as you like.
But not one flower placed on a holiday,
Will give them a single breath of new life.

You can talk to their headstone,
And hope that better days will come.
You might find that your grief is eased,
But I promise you that they will not respond.

I'm just hipping you to this sad truth—
Death is the common denominator.
Get busy loving the living, now,
So you won't regret your decision not to, later.

Family Who?

I can't say that patriarchal family ties
Were strained and, later, became severed.
It would be simpler to admit,
That they existed, never.

A family full of cousins—
Branches came from five sprouts of the vine.
Sadly, love from aunts and cousins
Was for something I longed, but would never find.

My mother was a proponent for right;
Reason and logic was what she spoke.
She wanted us familiar and close to family—
Not just hers but, too, my daddy's folks.

Whether a Christmas dinner
Or a simple walk to the store,
Any time family was present,
She made sure we were present and accounted for.

Over time, what I learned and plagued my mind—
Hurt the heart of the only son from their loving brother,
Was why my aunts' love for my sis and me,
Never amounted to that given for all of the others.

Was I looking at it wrong?
Had I been the one who was tripping?
What had brought all of this on?
Was there something that I was missing?

It shouldn't have come as a surprise to me;
I guess wanting love made me refuse to
See that they allowed older cousins to ridicule me,
Because I was different than what they were used to.

My folks scuffled like everyone else—
It was common in my hometown;
But encouraged me to make good grades and be neat;
For that, big cuz would always put me down.

Referring to me as "white boy"
In each and every opportunity in passing;
With the rest of the family just laughing
And helping to encourage his antics.

We would hear chuckling as we knocked on the door,
And I would always wonder how
Y'all were in stitches before we entered,
But no one is laughing, now.

It seemed that, over the years,
Any perceived chagrin brought them grins;
I never experienced what people say,
When they say their cousins were their first friends.

From my alma mater,
They stayed only minutes away;
You think they helped to celebrate
The day that I walked across the stage?

I guess that I should have probably—
Since, already, armed with that knowledge—
Figured that it would be the same,
When I was first in the family to graduate from college.

Fair-Haired Child

Everything is a go, for sure;
Whatever he asks, they permit.
For what it is he asks,
Is the very thing he gets.

When they choose to speak to him,
There is no intention of him listening.
They give him many things,
But not one of them is discipline.

When he is told "no,"
His temper tantrums are automatic.
He cuts up in class,
And talks to adults in a fashion so erratic.

Nevertheless, with what he is given,
No other kid could ask for more.
Spoiling him has helped prove to make,
Him rotten to the core.

He has never known a tattered rag;
His threads are befitting a king.
They celebrate what should be expected—
So much undue adulation over little things.

Instead of correcting bad behavior,
And coming down on him, fast,
They pat him on the back and are glad,
When, in class, he has barely passed.

Manhood Manifesto

I'm confident that
If men chose to rise and be men, again,
Women could just be women,
And children could be kids, again.

If we are talking about it,
Let's at least try and keep it real;
Single parenting can be done, because it is,
But it is really not ideal.

Mamas steadily knocking hustles—
Making a way, on top of a full-time job.
When she laid down to make the baby,
She wasn't alone so didn't have to work as hard.

No matter what she had—
Whether it was a son or a daughter.
She had a helping hand,
Because, then, she had a willing partner.

So since you chose to have your cake,
It's time to eat it like you ought to.
Though glamorized in society,
There's no honor in being a phantom father.

Giving just because you are garnished,
And spending time whenever you feel.
With disregard to how your kids are raised,
Or how their mama struggles when it's time to pay bills.

Time to step up your best efforts, brother;
Change what it is that you believe.
You aimed to be the man in terms of ladies;
Play it straight—that baby didn't choose to be conceived.

Maybe your choice to be a 'hot boy'
Is what got you on the hot seat.
But there is no need to compound it
By willfully choosing to be a deadbeat.

Sons need to learn to stand up for self,
But that words, too, can calm dissension.
In spite of what you hear or read,
Boys, too, can and do have daddy issues.

They will emulate their father's molds—
A lens lent toward the world's things and how to see them.
And for daddy's little girls,
He is the first example of how men should treat them.

Twice to Think

He is a little perplexed and vexed;
See he sees things backward through his eyes.
He has himself a full-time girl;
What do you know— he has a wife on the side.

It's evident that he ought,
To make the time to pay.
A first or second thought,
Of what is in right in front of his face.

He parades around his mistress—
Gives a scandal to the town.
Makes Wifey a joke to her sorority sisters—
She's a fool for how it's going down.

Faithful from the start,
She helped to mold him into a man.
Not as crazy as she seems—
You see, she, herself, too, has a plan.

Sitting quietly by as he lives the playboy life,
Always on the town—spending big at bars.
His lovely wife encourages him to celebrate his wealth,
By buying a bigger home and his deserved luxury cars.

The wife's been there since before the cash came;
It was her motivation that had helped to build him.
When none other would give him any attention, she was his all;
So a pre-nup was nothing he'd considered.

She is the one who manages their finances;
So she has the bank statements and credit card receipts.
Enough for her to prove his midnight creeps,
And give the court proof of his constant infidelity.

Weekly and almost daily, she has taken humiliation;
But the man will, soon, see his cash flow like a funneling frustum.
When the judge rules, from the bench, that the wife,
Should live a lifestyle to which she has become accustomed.

The Culture We Cultivated

We say we didn't reinvent the wheel,
So we never really decided.
That that's the way that things would be;
It was already like this when we got it.

I won't argue with that reasoning;
We did inherit it the way that they gave it.
But, somewhere along the line,
It was our hands that helped to cultivate it.

I'm not gonna talk in cryptic code,
Or use riddles or parables to make you wait.
I am talking about a culture of bullying,
And aim to tell it to you straight.

Though subconscious and not malicious,
There wasn't necessarily ill-meant intent.
But though we didn't invent it,
We did very little to end it.

Think of how we learn to play the dozens,
Using "joaning" to handle playground dealings.
Seemingly, using quick wits for joking,
Could quickly turn to someone ending up with hurt feelings.

Clothes, shoes and circumstances were material for the minute;
Dead relatives and mamas were all that were off limits.
But imagine feelings of the loser, after they had left;
Having little to do with their living; they didn't clothe themselves.

Then, there is the kid, not athletically inclined,
Who constantly hears it, because he rides the pine.
Maybe not taking lunch money, but it affects his self-esteem,
Always made to wonder, "Is EVERYONE better than me?"

Or the homely little girl who says that it's not fair,
That Grandmama won't ever allow her to go anywhere.
It probably would mean less and not add on to her tears,
If it didn't come with all the jokes and jeering of her peers.

Do we end the cycle?
No; we let it go on.
And to take the venom out,
Saying that it is just some harmless fun.

Many times, what happens—
And it is just as bad.
The person laughs at themselves,
So they won't be further laughed at.

Christmas Time Critiques

As of today, Christmas has come and gone,
But if we're blessed, it may, to us, come again.
So I hope that we will take
A few moments to look within.

What has become a trending topic,
Is Jesus's birth date accuracy.
But one thing I hope we take from the story,
Is what's needed but many may fail to see.

Too many times, we are lost in the hype;
The purpose becomes totally materialistic.
And what we should take away,
Becomes so distant that we might have missed it.

We take a one way to the poor house—
Unnecessarily willing to chase excessive debt.
All in order to impress the rest,
With such a meaningless bar that has been set.

"I've got to get my kids this thing,
So they will know that I love them.
And if, by chance, I can't afford it,
Their peers will find ways to judge them."

What someone may or may not say is on them;
Their opinions could be very varied.
I mentioned it in the context of Christmas since
Consider what they MUST have said about the Virgin Mary.

(Sadly...)

You know I ain't lying;
You know exactly how we do.
They probably ridiculed his mother, then;
Today, their ancestors are asking "What Would Jesus Do?"

They probably lent unsolicited opinions,
And even said that she was fast.
Not knowing the significance,
Of the baby that she was preparing to have.

Looking at the circumstances,
They probably saw claims of having not known a man as not true.
She was not carrying secrets,
But the savior of mankind within her womb.

In keeping Christmas or anything else in mind—
If you find that you need motivation—
Care less about what folks say,
And seek God's plan for the situation.

I Want Best for You

If you hear that, after years of fighting,
I have lost the battle to survive.
Or unexpectedly and out of the blue,
I took sick and suddenly died.

Or if you beat me out of the door,
It'll be bad enough if I have to be without you.
It would help my hurt to heal,
If I did not have to worry about you.

In just an instant and, many times, without notice,
We all go to whatever will be our forever home.
There is no such thing as a purgatory;
Once we are gone, we're gone.

Before we go any farther,
I think that I need to be clear.
Regardless to how I feel, no judge lives here—
It is only love that lives here.

There has never been a better treasure,
That I have seen with these two eyes.
If I were to see seventy years in this current life,
It would not nor could compare to eternity in paradise.

Sure, there is present suffering,
But I would not exchange it for a single second.
With what is waiting for me—
The treasures that are stored up for me in Heaven.

There is nothing special about me;
I am just the embodiment of prayers whispered, silently.
Side eye to the lies—it is not I;
I know that it is God who is inside of me.

Never has it been my kindness prompting His lovingkindness;
His love, I cannot comprehend.
He does not just allow me to contend;
He makes provisions for me to win.

That is why I am coming to you, now;
Everything that I have said is true.
I hope that you will believe on Jesus, too;
My friend, I just want what's best for you.

Her Name is 'Whosoever'

I think that there is much that can be debated,
But we can agree on one thing—
No matter your stead in life—whether believer or denier—
Many have heard of John, Three Sixteen.

Within the passing of the passage,
There's much there if you are just willing to explore.
We see, clearly, because of love,
What God gave, and who He gave it for.

We learn the reach of His love,
And that it's not reserved for select ones.
The word says, "For God so loved the world,
He gave His only begotten son."

The B clause of the scripture,
Is where I will set my sights.
It says, "That whosoever believeth in him should not perish,
But have everlasting life."

(Meet my friend...)

Pam has a bad drug problem;
She will steal and sell anything in sight.
If it will mean she will get to see the glow,
Come from the glass as she hits the pipe.

She lost her children to the system,
Before they were old enough to learn her name.
The judge terminated her parental rights,
After determining that she would never change.

Rehab back to crack house,
Is what has come to become her pattern.
I tell her she will get through it,
Because, to my God, it doesn't matter.

Whosoever was given hope,
Of a fruitful future and things getting better.
Sis is tired; Sis is in pain,
But Sis is who is meant by 'whosever.'

Many times, it's we as Christians who miss it—
Opportunities that come across our paths.
We poor salt into an open wound,
Instead of applying the good news as a healing salve.

We can become so highly religious—
So pompous in relying on appearances and buildings—
Overlooking if we take the spirit of Jesus with us,
He will show up for house calls to visit the afflicted.

(Let me introduce you...)

Drea has a banging body,
So she has chosen to strip.
She spins and claps and splits on the main stage,
But will turn tricks in VIP if they can tip.

She has Brazilian bundles, pushes luxury pedals in red bottoms—
Her face is "beat" with expensive makeup and fluttering lashes.
There is no mistaking the money she makes,
Or the fat checks that she cashes.

Promiscuity since a young age—
Sex is what she is ever-ready for.
Reputation is less than stellar,
She has always been known as an easy bed and more.

All everyone sees are her open legs;
They assume and judge and allege it's her.
When really it all stems from her mother's failure
To protect a young Drea from a predator.

Pain so deep, she numbs it with sex—
She can see, from what she knows, an end coming, never.
All she needs is for someone to tell her,
That she is a part of the "whosoever."

We have got to do a better job,
Of showing that Christianity is not an exclusive social club.
That it is to the least of us,
That God wants to show His love.

Laying our souls bare,
Declaring that it was God's intention,
For these and other captives to be set free;
All it takes is belief for Him to love and defend them.

But we can't bring them into the fold,
If we keep on hesitating.
We need to teach that "whosever" has a face,
And for them, Jesus has a makeover waiting.

Rest in the Lord

The Hem

Imagine the sea of surrounding people;
The Bible describes it as a "throng."
A densely-packed group of folks,
Crowding Jesus as He passed along.

Having given all of her money,
Not on habits—but things much purer.
For the issue of blood that plagued her for twelve years,
She only wanted for there to be found a cure.

When it came to trying Jesus,
Did she think, "I might as well?"
She had tried what is supposed to get results,
And found what's commonplace had failed.

While all of the others jockeyed for position,
Perhaps to encounter Him face-to-face,
She only aimed to touch the clothes He wore—
Faithful that that would supply her needed grace.

Completely aware of the happenings,
And not distracted by all of those who rushed Him,
Jesus felt some of His power leave His body—
Signaling to Him that someone had touched Him.

She could have just denied it,
And blended into the crowd that had been growing.
But she chose to own up to her intentions,
And told Jesus the details of her story.

Wanting nothing in return—
There was no basket to pass or plate to fill up.
He simply spoke to the woman,
Assuring that her faith had healed her.

Let this, for us, stand as a lesson;
No need for superficial things to please us.
The deliverance we need could come in an instant,
If we will just steal a way and reach to Jesus.

The Cost of the Cup

Eyes so battered, He can hardly see;
His body is beaten and worn.
Imagine the headache that He must have;
His body is adorned with a crown of thorns.

Abused—He has been so abused;
For their chance to do more, the crowd is jockeying.
They spit and hurl insults at Him—
His majestic essence, they are, steadily, mocking.

They've tried to strip His dignity—
Humiliate the spirit of His soul.
They've put vinegar on His open wounds,
And taken away His royal robe.

They've hit Him with everything they had—
Even pierced Him in His side.
Made Him deliver the cross to the place,
On which He was to be crucified.

The cost of the cup passed to Him,
Was high, and His charged to keep was hard.
Having the ability to save Himself,
He chose not to in order to fulfill the will of God.

Not only did He stand in my stead,
Take the charge and, also, do my time.
He was sentenced to an undue death;
They murdered an innocent man, for I would do the crime.

It was I who chose, freely, to sin,
Not always having had a changed heart for all my days.
But allowing my heart to purge,
Choosing to believe in His salvation cleanses all of my sins away.

The good news is of His grace,
And we should all learn and tell.
The very son of God, Himself,
Came, hung, bled, died, and rose to keep us from hell.

If anyone tried to find a flaw in Him,
I am sure that they could show none.
He preached loving others as we love ourselves;
He did wrong to no one.

Though, I am perfect by no means—
Do not think that, mistakenly.
I just have to thank Jesus for paying my debt of sin;
Thank you Lord for saving me!

Trier of Facts

It's better to put faith in God than trust in man;
No guessing—what He says will be is always exact.
No judgments matter except what He hands down;
He is the one true trier of facts.

When He tells me what I shall have and see,
To myself, I say, "That is that."
I cannot oppose He who holds the world in His hands;
He is the trier of facts.

Never do I question His words—
Even if I don't agree—with what He reveals or of its fit for me.
I know not enough about how I will get through the storm,
While He created and controls the humidity.

If man tries to tell me about anything past now,
And attempts to sell it off as prophecy,
I treat it like exactly what it is—
It's just his prospective to me.

If this life has taught me anything,
It's I had better see what he said as opinion.
He has not enlightened insight,
Nor, over creation, does he have dominion.

Whatever is or is not to come,
God has the ultimate decision.
The enemy cannot even hope to do me harm,
If he does not, first, of my father, ask permission.

Battle-Tested

There's no need to send requests—
Now or then, there ain't no friendin' me.
Veiled so thinly, the enemy's attempts
Come through friends and those kin to me.

It is a must and this and thus,
Let's mention difference between them and me.
I'm making the choice to speak it plain;
The enemy wants to see the imminent end of me.

As I head ahead,
He would rather see me back.
Placing his temptations
And bad habits straight in my path.

Hoping I will pursue to have comfort,
In the place of constant lack,
He wants to sit back and laugh,
When I have fallen flat on my lower half.

Like "Harlem Nights'" beginning scene,
With the fella mad from not winning,
I want everything that I lost—
And everything that he took in.

There is no running as remedy for me;
Tucking tail is not my common tendency.
As long as God strengthens and puts wind in me,
There'll be no intermingling contingencies.

Not ever will I let unsurety and doubt
Have the power to make a slave of me;
Instead, when it seems as if there is no way,
It will become a stage for me.

Not blocking my scope's crosshairs,
When there are things at which I aim to be.
Not afraid to navigate troubled waters,
Because my captain made the sea.

To the sky is where I will point my eyes—
No dimming lights by taking dismay.
The day may come when I am to stand and die on a hill,
But today won't be that day.

On a mission to show that being steadfastly faithful
Is, in no way, bogus,
No contrition to concentration,
Proving that focus is more than mere hocus pocus.

Way in the Wilderness

I thank the Lord that, through His grace,
He was merciful enough to save me.
Otherwise, what I've seen in these streets,
Would have driven me to the grave or, surely, run me crazy.

Too mean to die and not fit to live—
His grace was a true gift of blessing.
I can only attribute it to the Holy Spirit,
Who was always there to help me pass my testing.

(I say…)

After a lot of time spent in thought and prayer,
I believe that I have the riddle solved.
You can be who you are, just not be who you were,
In order to see the product of what Jesus has evolved.

Signed and sealed with His precious blood,
He delivered me like I was an important piece of mail.
God is and has been my way in the wilderness;
So there is no need for me to leave a paper trail.

(Listen…)

You've gotta put some action behind those words you speak,
Or forget everything that you are saying about it.
From that thing, if you don't have faith in being delivered,
Ain't no need in you steadily praying about it.

As the world hurls temptations at me,
It is He who helps me to resist them.
And any of my flesh's desired bad behaviors,
His power allows me to cease and desist them.

I am in no way even close to perfect,
But thank God I don't do all the things that I used to.
It is such a relief to me, every time that I think,
Every saint has a past, but every sinner has a future.

Above Reproach

Sunday school kids will tell you,
About the coat of many colors.
Then, the adults will remember how
He was sold into slavery by his brothers

How he and young Benjamin had their fathers favor,
Because they were birthed from another mother.
But my aim is to make it plain;
His integrity produced results like none other.

Could you imagine telling your siblings about a vision,
That they would bow before you, one day?
And after having to be persuaded not to kill you,
They put you in a pit and, then, made you a slave?

That would be something straight out of a movie, huh?
And beyond anything you've heard or seen.
Well, it happened to Joseph,;
And it happened when he was only seventeen.

Jealousy and spite made his brothers detest him,
And blinded them enough to make them try to best him.
Thank God He is not like the likes of men;
In His sovereignty, He chose to bless him.

Joseph could have looked at the situation,
And, easily, become down and out.
But he maintained his integrity,
And was soon put in charge of Potiphar's house.

Though his master looked at him,
And had to see that God was with him and in the plan,
Potiphar's wife looked upon young strapping Joseph,
And saw an attractive and virile man.

Daily, she propositioned him,
Having no intentions to play with him.
She had long since made up in her mind,
That she wanted him to stay so she could lay with him.

She grabbed hold of him in order to force him;
He ran away with no intention of going back.
With his garment in hand, she lied on him after he ran;
He was jailed as a result with his integrity still intact.

Tossed in with the other prisoners,
Who had found themselves in there,
Joseph found favor with the jailer,
And was entrusted with all of their care.

Understanding of dreams they had dreamed—
It seemed they could not get it.
Until with his interpretation,
Joseph said one servant would be restored and the other beheaded.

For making sense of the dream,
Joseph only requested one small favor—
That the cupbearer would remember Joseph,
After being returned to Pharaoh's good graces.

You might think he would remember such a gesture;
But the Pharaoh's cup bearer so soon forgot.
And so as for young Joseph,
He was left in the jail to rot.

Soon, the time would come,
When Joseph would see reprieve and be redeemed,
As he was finally remembered and called upon,
To interpret the Pharaoh's dream.

Because of his knowledge of surplus and famine,
And his in-depth analysis and description,
Joseph gained the favor of Pharaoh,
Being made governor because God must have been with him.

Who could have imagined,
What God had planned for this man?
After 13 years, all except Pharaoh's meals were in his hand;
Joseph was second most powerful in all the land.

After they had languished in guilt and anguish,
When having to go to Joseph for supplies of food,
Mercifully, he told them that all was forgiven;
What they had meant for bad, God had intended for good.

Help Coming Down

When I was just a child,
And standing not many inches from the ground,
I would hear the old preachers preach,
And say that they felt their help coming down.

Time after time, I would give it thought—
So interested, so I would always ponder.
But as I grew, I prayed, meditated, and read,
So I wouldn't have to wonder any longer.

As time passed, I learned just what those preachers meant;
I was blessed to learn and see.
During days that I felt I was drained and spent,
It was the Holy Spirit moving in me.

In times when it seemed as if my wick's end was close,
And things could get no harder,
I would feel a sudden chill and have sudden strength—
Just enough to push a little bit farther.

(What I've learned...)

The psalmist said to look to the hills for my help,
Because my help comes from the Lord.
So I know that if I lift my eyes to Him,
My needs not only can, but shall be heard.

There is no estimated time of resolution,
Or expiration time for which problems to stay.
But I can rest assured and believe, in faith,
That, somehow, help will be on its way.

We don't have to look in terms of bible times;
Even today, it can be translated.
Jesus made it plain that He would never leave us,
Nor would He ever forsake us.

He explained that He had to leave,
In order that He could send the Comforter.
In the person of the Holy Spirit—
There to protect us when we feel nothing under us.

He always goes ahead before us,
To clear the path of toils and snares.
In the midst with us as we step,
He also seals the rear after we have left from there.

God is omnipresent—always there,
And all-knowing—He is truly omniscient.
So, like the Apostle Paul says,
His grace is more than enough and surely sufficient.

The Twins

Nowhere in my bible have I ever read,
That life would ever be easy.
Jesus promised that if I'd receive Him,
He would never leave me.

Some use this term off-based;
They are just proficient in talking.
But, seriously, I have been pursued by two,
That are very proficient in stalking.

There are things of which I am certain—
That I choose to trust with all of me.
The psalmist said with certainty,
That surely Goodness and Mercy shall follow me.

(I've seen it…)

It was in my darkest hour,
They reminded me that there could be light.
Because when you've been doing wrong so long,
You think that it is what right feels like.

Sometimes, we do things in routine—
Even if detrimental, we rehearse.
If right had been done, at first,
There would be no bad to worse and no curse to reverse.

Many people will tell you,
"Boy, I sure was lucky; I dodged a bullet, too."
I know enough to believe in the hand of God,
As He looks after babies and fools.

And when I was too stupid,
To care of how I would fare,
They stood as avenging angels,
In charge of and charged with my care.

With such passion and enthusiasm,
They have been present with blazing fire.
As not to disappoint his words,
Or make the psalmist look like a liar.

When fast living had me so raggedy,
And I was blinded by the fun,
They picked me up and clothed me,
With God's armor, for the battle that was to come.

But thank the Lord for His provision,
So that sin hasn't found and swallowed me.
Like the psalmist, there are twins assigned;
Surely, Goodness and Mercy follow me.

(I say…)

In times of trouble,
When peril was, surely, certain,
They stepped in as surrogates,
In order to bear my heavy burdens.

When I was praying to get,
Instead of, in my getting, to get understanding,
They let death leave my ghost behind my door post,
And the law without reprimanding.

Whether the jealous boyfriend,
Or the man feeling cheated because of gambling figures,
It was only Goodness and Mercy sent by God,
That could have calmed their itching trigger fingers.

Not just by brushes with potential death,
Look at how you have side-stepped hunger.
What a miracle your ends met, once again,
Or your old car rolled on a little longer.

Did you think it was something that you did—
Maybe an act, righteous in your eyes?
Doing good is great, but don't be mistaken;
God is who gives you your means to survive.

My reason in mentioning this,
Is because we might look and find ourselves aghast,
If we stop complaining while wishing for what we want,
And be thankful for all of the things that we have.

Keep Going

Worth a Cuss

Some of us worked nerves, of course,
And readily heard the fuss.
But there were some with purpose unearthed
Who were not really worth a cuss.

It's been said and said 'til run in the ground;
I am sure you have heard the story.
They say when the coach doesn't correct you,
Is when you should begin to worry.

Sad to say, but I was one of the guys
Who they cared less if I kicked up dust.
Anytime I did not get it right,
I guess they figured I wasn't worth a cuss.

They hardly ever pushed and prodded;
It seemed they didn't care if I didn't heed what they'd say.
In my opinion, it was simple to them;
They just wouldn't let me play.

In this scenario and others similar,
Does the chicken or egg come first?
Did their choice to not invest in my best,
Help to make me grow better or worse?

Waiting on My Ride

My wife jokes with me, often—
Saying that I would like to die "great."
My response, each time, is I don't aim to die great;
I just don't have to die late.

It is motivation, each day,
That I am here and in all I give,
That when I am dead and gone,
They would know that I had lived.

I see the signs of the end of times;
I can't wait to vanish and take to the sky.
While some focus on fake news and reality fun facts,
I am getting my packs and waiting on Jesus to come back.

I want to set my house in order
Like Hezekiah when allowed to—
Without boasting and celebrating my righteousness,
Like many of the proud do.

Pouring into lives of others,
Even if it often meant emptying me.
Believing, daily, that anything
That was meant for me would be.

Crying in silence when heartache got violent,
And love seemed so lost to me.
Presented as refreshing while dealing with depression—
Not speaking of it, just writing off the cost to me.

Revelations in this nation—
Promises not holding true.
Disappointed in the attack of brown and black,
While many are screaming they will back the blue.

Sad knowledge in the fact that
Agencies are taking babies away from day to day
Unjust in separating families,
While other mothers don't want their own babies, anyway.

Big Brother, I

Why must I constantly answer for mistakes of others?
And provide the things they lack?
Is it essential I be big brother to the world—
Bearing this cross on my weary back?

I play the cards that were dealt to me,
And always attempt to do my best,
To help all around me and, then,
Extend to help all the rest.

My eyes burn from exhaustion,
And my body aches from wear.
And my back has grown sore,
From the aforementioned cross that I must bear.

I am screaming to the jailer,
"Let me go! Let me free!"
The hurt, I can manage,
But I wish they would simply let me be.

I will not abort my struggle,
Against the resistance of the locks.
Nor will I feel inferior against their pistols,
Though they are aimed and already cocked.

I pick up my fists,
Just as far as they can go.
While contemplating on the punch,
That I know that I must throw.

Strong to the Finish

Forced to sleep at night, and face the waking day,
I etched my name in stainless steel, and still I made my way.
Through the passing present, my eyes were forced to see,
A new beginning of what's to come—what the future held for me.

The evils were present, and the rewards were hid,
But I stayed away from becoming a skid.
Row to the world, and to my family, a disgrace,
Never failing to recognize, God's everlasting grace.

They pushed me and pulled me, they bowed me and stole me,
All I wanted was for someone, to love me and hold me.
I did what I could and righted my wrongs,
Though small in stature, I still fought strong.

One day I will be the last dog left,
In my purple and gold, and stomping my steps.
I will have my degree, I'll be makin' my pay,
I'll have my goal achieved, I will be Dr. J.

Fight of My Life

Like spy movies from the past,
The warning was less subtle than abrupt.
In no unclear terms,
I knew that this message may self-destruct.

Battle with tobacco,
Fight with fornication,
Duel with depression,
Iconic bout with indignation.

A speed bump to hungry stomachs,
It's stress relieving therapy that fits in my pocket.
Packed tightly in a puck,
As if, maybe, I might play hockey.

This all on the heels of and after,
Something else that was shown to me.
No smells of smoke stacks;
I chose clove squares that smelled like potpourri.

Wasn't much for that sticky,
For fear it would leave my pee so cloudy.
So I pulled and dragged until I could see clearly,
How to make my family proud of me.

How to sidestep allegations of hazing—
And other issues I was charged to fix.
Like things I'd learned from explicit flicks,
And done with ready and willing chicks.

All the while, keeping so many secrets,
That I would not dare to tell.
With the knowledge that some of those closest to me,
Had made it plain that they'd hoped I'd fail.

I kept a smile so bright like a shining light,
Making like, all the time, that all was well.
Thinking that this was the fight of my life,
And I had not heard the final bell.

Executive Order

Maybe there's something someone, before,
Gathered and came back and told you.
Regardless, what you see, when you look at me,
Is in the eye of the beholder.

No matter if in rugged jeans,
Or, perhaps, in pleated slacks,
You'll either see a beat-up shirt,
Or a corporate tie to match.

Like the stride of a sniper's rifle,
Or the shiny sharpened blade of a machete,
I try and leave lasting impressions,
So you won't, easily, forget me.

When our encounter is behind us,
I hope that I will have left you with,
A feeling from our dealing,
Like I could carry the title of "the executive."

I've grown confident in creative company—
Willing in my working.
I treat it like my desk,
Handling business through cellular service.

See about it in the present tense—
Address tomorrow's business just because.
Anybody that knows me knows,
You get 'er done when you give me a buzz.

Patient as I go through life,
There's no need to live it livid.
I'm hardly ever in a hurry,
Especially when I am handling business.

In the unforeseen event,
That my skills should dare deceive me,
My thoughts will always remain,
The want to learn and will to win will never leave me.

Better Than Ever

I understand that self-pity's a show,
That no one wants to see.
There is no honor in settling;
Complacency has no place on the mantelpiece.

I've just got to get out the kinks and quirks;
I have to work out all of the bugs.
I don't wanna be more than I am;
I'd just like to be better than I was.

It is pointless for anyone
To ever try and predict my demise.
'Cause ten toes down,
I'm he who declares that I shall rise.

I've never been the one,
Who is satisfied with words like "can't."
I'm always hard to the paint,
And my heart's holler is never growing faint.

My eyes won't bulge out of my head,
Until my belly's fatter than a frog.
Because I'll chase my dreams and hunt them down,
Like a steadfast bloodhound dog.

I'm gonna keep on striving
And keep on striding—
Gotta believe I'm alive,
So I'll, soon, be arriving.

Chest of Treasure

It is not the fear of failure—
Rather, the fever to flourish that makes me swell.
Not prideful, but maybe my pride will make me,
CEO like on "ATL."

I have had a taste of success,
So, with it, I often flirt.
I feel like I'm two-timing my wife,
Because I'm married to my work.

Mind's far from closed from worldly exposure,
But never off of my humble beginnings.
I use what I have learned, thus far,
To make for a better ending.

What is to come will, by leaps and bounds,
Surpass the things that I have seen.
I already have a treasure chest,
And didn't have to look on the floor of the sea.

Old Soul

I'm gonna search until I find it—
Even until nothing is left in me.
I don't expect to find coins in a box—
Just knowledge and sweat equity.

Goin' to Town

It is no secret that I have a love for words;
Here is just a peep at how I let them convey.
Because written words remain and are remembered,
When life's winds wisp spoken words away.

Like a fisherman when crashing waves,
Bring a haul in with the tide.
Or a relay sprinter coming out of the curve,
Leaning in to catch his stride.

Much like rollin' around, in summertime,
In a freshly washed and waxed and shining car.
Like T'Challa's mother screaming to him from the waterfall,
It's where you get to show them who you are.

I bend and back and up, again—
Taking pages from "The Matrix."
Inserting a pause to show drawing breath,
I hasten up my cadence.

(Like this…)

It is how I lead into now—
There is no need to wait 'til later;
It is an opportunity to whet your appetite,
And set your palate for my flavor.

Like a hook before the chorus in R&B,
It walks you into the coming words.
It is where I choose to smile so bright,
Because it is time to shine through verbs.

Cost of Admission

Regardless of the direction of your adventure,
Or which path you choose to explore,
There will always be a price to pay,
In order to get you through the door.

True; not everything that is increased,
Will come to you as result of a loss.
But you have unreasonable reasoning,
If you don't think you will pay the cost to be the boss.

(Think about it...)

An athlete may have talent,
But that is not significant enough alone.
The game is where he makes the newspaper,
But the gym and grind are where he makes his bones.

College scholars may make big dollars,
Once they've graduated and begun to work.
But the opportunity would never come,
If they did not have the long nights of study, first.

Don't overlook everyday opportunities,
Or attempt to take them for granted.
Failure to plan will have you, ultimately,
Planning to come up short-handed.

In every instance,
There is a place for a lesson.
But you will never ever get a second chance
To make a first impression.

So seize it when presented—
Attack it when you get it.
Know that what seems to be nothing, today,
May, one day, be your cost of admission.

Make Yesterday Jealous

Be thrilled as you live;
Let each daybreak make you zealous.
Make the new day great on purpose—
Make the choice to make yesterday jealous.

On worthless things, do not rely;
Put foolish pride aside.
Make up your mind that you will be not be denied;
Crest the wave and ride the tide.

Put in place the steps it takes;
Don't just settle with wishing predictions.
Work hard for what it is you want;
Do absolute best to enrich your vision.

Know that regardless of best laid plans,
Not everything will always go well.
When need be, draw strength from times,
When you tried but found that you failed.

For lands to be expanded,
Best effort is demanded.
Do not take for granted the very hand,
Of which you have been granted.

One Night Stan

He's been steadfast in his prayer life,
Talking with God and devising a plan.
Now, after many tried and failed attempts,
He is thankful for another chance.

Doors have been shut in Stan's face so much,
He has become accustomed to "no."
But each time, he has cried out,
"Lord, it's not my time—now, wither shall I go?"

He has been encouraged to give up hope,
In each instance of his testing.
Some have even suggested that,
Secret sin is the cause of his hindered blessings.

Stan has taken a stance of desolation in place of desperation;
His concentration and focus are laser like when he is alone.
No taking breaks or time away—
He has kept his nose close to the grindstone.

Whereas others would have given up hope,
Or at least they would have relented,
Stan made conscious efforts to better himself,
For when, again, with the chance he would be presented.

He made a vow within himself;
He wouldn't aspire to get to the next man's wealth.
Each day, he would trade good for better in pursuit of best,
Only grading against goals, some time ago, that he had set.

Finally, the time came, for his shot at fame—
It was his time to show and prove.
A charge to keep to his God—
To himself, he had nothing to lose.

So he took to the stage, and a war he waged—
Showtime had come, and he was on.
Time to hush up all the doubters,
And show the world that he belonged.

He did one for the ages;
There was no note that he couldn't hit.
He dazzled them with his soulful and raspy notes;
He wowed the crowd with his showmanship.

Finishing his set,
He left the audience wanting for more.
Not trying to but upstaging the headliner,
They all chanted for an encore.

On his way straight to the top,
It could be assumed and is, steadily, seeming,
All because he refused to stop believing in God and,
To himself, refused to stop dreaming.

Proposition Denied

His favor gave them vapors,
And, to some, a heightened fever.
Hate how I spend my leisure,
And may even give them fits of seizures.

And for what it's worth,
I chose not to accept affliction.
Putting my Father first,
I denied the devil's proposition.

Just like a freight train,
Rumbling down the tracks,
There ain't no hitting brakes,
And I ain't turning back.

No matter how much dap I've slapped—
How many women and children hug me—
That does not mean for a single minute,
That any of those people really love me.

Humbly, I can honestly say,
That I have never been worthy.
I've just been around this long,
Because He chose to show His mercy.

I have so much to delight in,
And am thankful for many reasons.
Please believe me when I say,
God is blessing me in seasons.

Having to get a handle on things,
Just not that of my sword.
I've found that no weapon I possess,
Is as mighty as the Lord.

So hold fast to what you think you know;
Keep on doing it your way.
Me, myself, I'll stick to what I know,
And keep my faith in Yaweh.

Not Deliberate

The people's movement—
I became a part of it.
Just like I was from,
The lineage of Spartacus.

Hardly made for analogy,
Or befitting of a parable.
Not deliberate like the smoke from a pipe,
Or gun blast from a barrel.

I know a whole lot of four-letter words,
And I use them more than plenty.
But my favorite four-letter word,
Is one that gives back to more than many.

It's a word called "hope,"
That a lot of people are lacking, these days.
It seems like only a few,
Are ones that get the joy and the praise.

So, my mission is to offer hope,
To the man standing on the corner.
Who gets up and goes to work, every day,
With more than the sales of marijuana.

Man, hope is a powerful thing;
It's a powerful word to say.
It can wipe out the cloudy skies, at night,
And brighten up the days.

But a lot of people don't have hope, now;
Cause times are hard, you see.
So I take the burden of hope,
And I put it all on me.

Lord, have mercy; the struggle's hard and,
Sometimes, it seems you can't go on.
But if I can just give a little hope,
I know my rights will replace my wrongs.

See, I'm from the bottom;
I've lived there; I've been there.
And when you're on the bottom,
It's kind of hard feeling you can win there.

I just wanna offer hope;
I wanna wrap it up and bind it.
I wanna give it to many and not confine it
And leave the world better than I find it.

Spreading Good News

Winning is winning,
But to lose is a bust.
Point shaving is cheating,
So one's best is a must.

I'm spreading good news,
Unlike the gentlemen on C-SPAN.
Lend ears; shed views;
And I will give you the game plan.

If shot correctly,
There's no chance that you will miss.
Success is coming, directly,
So listen to this.

My mother taught me,
To shed my childish obsessions.
My father taught me,
To breed my natural aggression.

No Need to Be a Peacock

Everything but everything—
I've never been a superstar.
Richer than a rich man,
With money long and fancy cars.

I never romanced all of the fancy,
Perks that came with the change in jobs.
And I passed on the chance to prance—
Like a bourgeoisie from the suburbs or snobs.

But who am I; what do I know—
Just a po' boy from the country.
And the ideal of being a hope dealer,
Was something that was thrust upon me.

It's in me, I feel it;
I know I can heal it.
If with nothing but my mind,
I know that I can will it.

I'm talking and rambling,
Trying to articulate my thoughts.
I believe in my heart, if I keep fighting,
The battle will be well-fought.

Soldier on life's battlefield,
But never just a killa man.
Always aware of the atmosphere,
I use it like a guerilla man.

I made up in my mind,
I would be too bad to beat.
Is that a nightlight in my bedroom,
Or me shining in my sleep?

Once again, you know it's me—
A self-fulfilling prophecy.
I've done good at what I said I would,
And am what I predicted to be.

Adversity always has a way,
To make things seem so real.
And that way either builds the skills,
Or succeeds to steal the will.

Maybe I'm just a dreamer;
Maybe nothing will ever change.
But at least I would've tried to make it better
For those on the road down which I came.

Going Yard

I had done some living,
But still was wet behind the ears.
I thank God for the fact,
That I had wisdom beyond my years.

I had been told of Normal's Hill,
But knew not what was really happening.
The closest I had seen until then,
Had been the Magic City Classic.

With everything except the kitchen sink,
Was what I would be taking.
Still, I had no idea for me,
Just what had been awaiting.

We headed up Four Thirty-One;
My brothers from home had done the same.
By the time I made it,
We had to move in in the pouring rain.

My parents and sister stayed until the next day;
In the city, they had to stay the night.
Lines in Financial Aid, the next day,
Were my intro to a new way of life.

They said that all tuition and fees,
Before starting class, must be paid.
Scholarship covered all but room and board,
Because of the mistake they had made.

It wasn't until we hit the yard,
After all of the parents had left.
That we saw our version of "A Different World,"
Of which we must, then, explore ourselves.

It was as if I had been clothed in darkness;
My eyes had really been closed.
I realized just how much to which,
I had not been exposed.

Many times, movie and tv screens,
Will make it seem like it.
Whenever black folks get together,
That there have to be riots or violence.

But what I saw with my own two eyes,
Was hard for me to come to grips with.
I remember thinking that,
"I'm glad I have four more years of this."

Imagine this if you will:
Opportunities for better futures, regardless of pasts.
Conscious of our culture—
Educated black folks with packs on backs.

Young adults carving out a niche—
No stereotypes of hustlers getting "paid."
Hair in every amazing texture—
Beauty abundantly in every shape and shade.

Camaraderie was always commonplace;
It was not anything outside of the norm.
Many nights, great bonds were formed,
By playing cards in common areas of dorms.

Do not get me wrong;
The love was not just among the cliques and factions.
The faculty and, too, the staff,
Managed to get in on the action.

It was more than just a job for them;
They wanted to make us better.
They were not just our teachers;
Instead, they were advocates and life helpers.

Just dapping up and laughing it up—
It was not an uncommon thing to speak.
A sea of the maroon and white—
Family reunion, seven days a week.

Shades of Soul

I love all of my people, but hey—
I am just speaking facts.
We embrace ignorance of the past,
By saying things like "she is a pretty black."

Each shade is equally essential—
Tells a story and plays its part.
Every complexion is a reflection,
Showing its own traces of the grace and the hand of God.

From Tracee Ellis to Tisha and Tachina
And all of the ladies of TLC.
Taraji to both of the Reginas—
"Hey auntie" to the magnificently fabulous Angela B.

To Taral and Ms. Sumpter,
Others can hardly compete.
Lupita , Danai and Viola are so fine,
They could all make the heart skip a beat.

No wonder their features are often featured;
No need to enshrine them—they are living sculptures.
Our creator never makes mistakes; in fact, with these and more,
He did it BIG for the culture.

I'm just saying not only a single shade equals beauty,
Like a single one doesn't equate to wrong.
There is heritage in all of it;
What is common among them is they are black and strong.

Forged from within the fire,
Her smile is one the strikes of life cannot take.
She has got a spirit about her
An abundance of money just could not make.

Her goals are not unlike those,
Set forth by her ancestors.
Evolved in ways over time,
But centered on her posterity having better.

Resilience is her brilliance—
Her strength is an undeniable fact.
No matter which shade decorates her,
She is unapologetically black.

Whatever her learned lessons or profession—
Even if motherhood might have missed her,
If she has drawn breath, she's somebody's black daughter;
Therefore, she is a black sister.

No matter her body type, she is the archetype;
She cannot be boxed in or handled.
Effortlessly, she's shifted the paradigm—
She is, now, society's standard.

Breaking barriers and shattering glass ceilings,
She no longer has an accepted "place."
She and her sisters are the face of the rainbow after a great storm;
Of their promise, we are blessed to have a taste.

This is a public service announcement to put all on notice,
And I hope that it is suitable.
Know that, though, the diversity of black is bountiful,
ALL BLACK IS ALWAYS BEAUTIFUL.

Sun-Ripened Fruit

She is a masterpiece,
From the moment that she wakes up.
It is always her choice to make,
But she has no need for any makeup.

Always build her up;
She has the whole world to bring her down.
Don't just compliment when convenient or often scream "Queen;"
Instead, do best to help adjust her crown.

What she means to those jeans,
Just cannot be refuted.
Grade A—no beef, just brains;
She is a stellar student.

Never will you hear her be,
Regarded as stupid.
She knows about prayer,
And she ain't afraid to use it.

(She shines…)

It's the blossoming of the buds
That teach us to protect her—
The welcome light of the day,
Softening her flesh and sweetening her nectar.

It's the kiss from the sun
That causes her skin to shine.
It's the refining process
That could only come with time.

Don't be fooled by her sweetness;
She has the strength of the rind.
Her spirit of replenishing
Brings springtime to mind.

A reflection of refreshment,
She is a perfect picture of patience.
She is the epitome of essence—
Personification of radiance.

Plain Perfection

Pretty, petite, and priceless—
Picture of good pedigree.
Confident but not arrogant,
Unquestionably, she is sexy to me.

The way that she walks—
Effortlessly, she seems to glide.
Feeling eyes facing forward,
Helping hands hanging at her sides.

Pouty little lips,
Always pose the perfect pucker.
No wonder she's emulated by sisters—
Infatuation to all the brothers.

No alley cats can hold a candle;
The big names can't quite compare.
It is her immaculate plainness,
That makes her beauty seem so rare.

And it is her humble upbringing,
That prevents and will not let her
Speak with an ungrateful tongue,
And that makes this girl look even better.

What a grateful gift to man,
If we will only learn her lessons.
Paying attention to her subtle beauty,
When fortunate enough to have her present.

Mocha Lightning

Fingerprints of Photoshop,
So often, tend to pollute the posts.
But I look for that mocha lightning;
It shows me that there has been some kind of growth

Some people fawn over skin and shapes;
Some are hypnotized by what's in the eyes.
I look at the cocoa-colored tiger stripes,
That may decorate breasts, hips and thighs.

Fashion models will always have their place—
There will remain a demand for their profession.
But, for me, there's something beautiful about stretch marks;
They show not just present beauty, but a pattern of progression.

Nothing manufactured by the artist's touch-up brush;
No manmade software or mouse clicks to try and wow.
Just elasticity of the skin that God gave,
To tell to the beholder's eyes of how.

She went from the days of a bumbling youngster,
And blossomed into the phase of budding young lady.
Her marks will stand as monuments—
Journal entries from when she's had her own babies.

Just like with the marks on her skin,
We see there has been some expansion and stretching.
I believe they are symbolic of how she can be more—
While constantly representing a natural essence.

Gray Hair, Grace Head

The wisdom of her crown is unmatched;
Not a lot of others even come close.
She may not have a single black hair left;
Almost completely gray, she has more than most.

When she brushes her silver locks,
Through her curls, the brush just glides.
Most times, when you see her,
She has it braided—beside her face, one adorning either side.

As her peers have aged, they chose
To dye theirs and turn it back black.
But even when hers turned, prematurely,
She always saw gray hair as a badge.

Not a Bible thumper in any sense,
But she is fluent in the word.
And so she considers her gray as a crown,
And extended time—a blessing from the Lord.

The Bible is quite clear when it says,
Children's children are a crown to old men.
She believes that her gray is a promise kept;
It is no sneaky coincidence.

Natural disasters have passed her;
The rolling hearse's wheels and illness have missed her.
And if she lives to see the coming twins,
Her children's children will have their own grandchildren.

Oh, but how she knows she's blessed!
It makes her full when she looks around.
Still able to live alone and fix meals,
What reason could she possibly have to frown?

The Greatest is the Latter

Love will get us through our hardships,
And comfort us in pain.
Urge us through our arguments,
No matter who is to blame.

It will end the groaning stomach of hunger—
Being a filling morsel to swallow.
And always shine as a glimmer of hope,
When clouds are forecast for tomorrow.

It's the tidbits of joy that we get,
When life's misfortunes come through and surprise us.
And when we struggle to make it through,
It will be there to revive us.

Like finding delight in movie night,
Or picnics in the park.
They say love will not keep the lights turned on;
That's fine; I'll just love you in the dark.

It does not falter and never fails;
No sprint—It's always a marathon.
The bad of some times faintly pale,
Against the good ones in comparison.

If we learn to not mind the time,
Then, nothing else will matter.
The good book says that of faith, hope, and love,
The greatest is the latter.

Jordan Is A-callin'

He looks as if he is ready
And has no interest on intending,
To ask for a little longer,
So his number of winks will be extended.

And in this current battle,
He has been a good contender.
But, now, knows the fight is ending,
And death will be here in a minute

He had done best to prepare his family,
Because experience taught him this type of loss is hard.
He has given final instructions,
And he has made his peace with God.

From the oldest to the youngest—
Presence of children and grandchildren was what he requested.
Like the fathers of ancient times,
He wanted to bestow on them a blessing.

Now, death's rattle has made his speech seem like babble,
And his eyes are set and fixed in space.
It seems as if his mind is many miles away;
It's as if he is in another place.

For days, he's been talking about deceased loved ones,
As if they were within reaching range.
At those moments, he smiled so brightly;
His expression, in this moment, has not changed.

Without warning, his grip goes limp;
His surrounding family sobs while he lies peaceful.
The angels had returned for him,
To usher him into the presence of Jesus.

Hunter Johnson Presents…

Mother Wit

Come at Once

I know the feeling all too well,
And I can say that it is far from fun.
The voice on the other end of the phone saying,
"If you plan to come, you'd better come at once."

For my great-grandmother, great-uncle and grandfather,
I was made aware so that I could come.
Though as not to alarm me so I could drive,
I even received the call about my mom.

Anxiety takes over your mind—
Memories as your loved one is knocking on Heaven's door.
You try to stay calm while anticipation makes you
Heavily, press the pedal, steadily, to the floor.

Pictures rush and mix and mesh—
A collage from all the years.
And no matter how you try to fight,
You succumb to salt-drenched tears.

And no matter how all of those thoughts gut punch you,
And take a hold of your mind,
The one thought that is front and center,
Is "Lord, please just let me make it in time."

'Neath the Daisies

Although I knew I must,
Trust, I could not find the words to say it.
So, I'm depending on my pen and pad,
To help to try and convey it.

The terms of our endearment,
Are often quoted, but seldom heard.
But who really knows the power—
The depth of this simple word?

Some things, to some, are entitled,
So give it all to them.
Express your deepest sentiments,
With each recall of this acronym.

Father And Mother,
I Love You
Give them their flowers, while they live,
And are there to stand and hug you.

Tell them you love them, often;
Pay homage for your raising.
So you will not be regretful,
When they are resting 'neath the daisies.

The Common Denominator

When you look at a table,
The centerpiece is from where all items flow.
Just like the baseline of a song,
It is what keeps the beat after setting the tone.

The same can be said in the same way,
About a family's matriarch or patriarch.
They set the direction and function as the center;
In a word, they are the heart.

There never is a question,
As to where everyone is going to be.
It is understood without needing to be stated;
Granny's house is where we all will meet.

Everyone is welcome;
Everybody comes if they are able.
Aging children wait their turns,
To be promoted up from the kiddie table.

Spend-the-night parties are impromptu;
Holiday gatherings are always a given.
Little children litter the landscape,
Knowing not to be sitting in the middle of grown folks' business.

But what happens so often,
When the beloved family head dearly departs,
The family that they hand-crafted and cherished
Is the very first thing that falls apart.

Since I have seen it happen,
I implore you to do yourself a favor.
Make sure there is someone to step in the gap,
And serve as common denominator.

Someone to serve as reporter—
A hub and keeper of family tree, documents and pictures.
Someone to preserve the record,
Serving as historian in the continuing oral tradition.

A planner and organizer,
Who can calibrate everyone's schedule to fit the season.
And make sure getting together is feasible,
When before, you all never needed a reason.

To protect your firmly-planted family,
These may be things you need to explore.
To avoid the void that often comes,
When your common denominator is no more.

Empath

When I say I got a feeling,
It's not a common cold or a shot of flu.
My path as an empath
Helps me to see things I never knew.

More than what I could know
Is not just a trick played by my mind.
A John Coffey of my day and time—
It's like their pains and joys are made into mine.

The joy that comes from pouring in—
Their secret, I know, but don't repeat it.
But like a battery, often times,
I find myself drained—my energy depleted.

For years, I knew not how to describe it—
Many times, to it, I had refusal.
Research is paramount in learning;
I thank God for giving me Google.

I thought that something was wrong with me—
Knowing people I barely knew far too well.
Before they would open up to me,
I could, to them, analyze and tell.

Something was not quite right;
I could help to solve the mystery.
Giving insights like a slight of hand,
I could run down their family history.

Ask the Answer

The depth of perception, can be deathly deceptive,
The mother of malice, and of unrest, quite receptive.
Killer of conscience, and sniper of all the notions,
Buddy to blunder, and steroid to all emotions.

To know is to say "no," to a life filled with horrors,
To the ghosts of the past, and the pains of tomorrow.
So the surest roadmap, to a car that's ever-driven,
Is ask for the answer and, to you, it shall be given.

The Same 24

If we looked for differences,
We could find plenty between you and me.
In terms of common ground,
We have the same when it comes to opportunity.

It takes just under 24 hours
For our earth to return to its rightful place.
Simply put in layman's terms,
That means we have the same 24-hour day.

True; our talents ain't the same;
You might accel where I'm not well.
But it's an even playing field
In that we have the same time to win or fail.

Though that's the common denominator and constant,
The variable of it is just this:
What we do or do not conquer
Hinges on what we do with it.

If you choose to spend your time
On the hunt and on the grind,
But I settle for settling
And waste what I have left of mine

Should I feel slighted by my plight
And want to give you a piece of my mind?
Or say that life's not fair
And be mad at you for choosing to brighten your shine?

If you put the muscle behind your hustle
And use every chance to make
Plans to gain an upper hand,
Should I break your spirit or decide I'm going to take

What you put sweat and blood into—
Should I feel entitled to success?
Even though I took what was given
And put forth much less than best?

If so, I am the worst kind of man;
I went for the okie doke.
I thought I would get participation trophies
And allowed myself to become a joke.

Now, I'm mad at you for making the best
Out of the cards that you were given.
Depressed about the way you dress—
Can't stand the way in which you're living.

Shine Box

When some folks think of a shine box,
Their mind's gears turn and spin—
Thinking of things like their bling bling,
Or what they place their jewelry in.

I can't say that that's my style;
It's not for me, myself.
The joy of my shine box,
Is drawn from somewhere else.

I like to take my time—
Iron my slacks until creases shine through.
And consider the look's success,
By how cuffs sit atop my shoes.

Now, I have no problems with suede;
I kind of like the mattes.
But I love the light hitting my kicks,
And them kicking it, right back.

(Dig This…)

I generously massage the saddle soap,
With hopes to cleanse the leather.
I know that, if shined while clean,
They will just shine that much better.

Some might overlook them,
And would rather not mess with,
But I give great attention
To give detail to every crevice.

I look at the leather,
As it contracts and expands.
I know it is working—
It's softening in my hand.

Once I am done with the cleaning,
I set the pair to the side.
Before I make my application,
I give them time to dry.

After I've gone and come back,
To give things time to settle,
I twist the can of Kiwi,
In order to loosen the lid on the metal.

With everything having dried,
And laces, now, removed,
I take a paper towel,
And smooth the polish upon the shoes.

I put it on a little thick;
I don't aim to make any waste.
In order to measure progress, later,
I'll need to see where shine replaces paste.

Then, I take to brushing—
Letting the brush's bristles hit them.
Replenishing the beauty that was there,
But had just been hidden.

I use a small cloth,
And buff them until they gleam.
My habits are due to what I've learned,
Because of what I have seen.

The best place that I have grabbed,
My lessons in living,
Is from those who came before me,
Who took care of what they had been given.

Stand and Speak

Call it hope for the future;
It's mixed with deference for the past.
It's on this grassy land
That I've chosen to stand and plant my flag.

There have been rumblings in the streets,
While the bowels of power have gone without beseech.
I stay consistent in delivery,
But, now, know that I must stand and speak.

Not for prospects of cashing checks;
I'll take the value of integrity, first.
I'm not taking any dictation,
If it's not within my agreed upon scope of work

But what I will lend my voice to,
Is those who are complicit in or implicitly trading right for wrong.
For that, I will give last even if gasping breaths—
No hesitation in making that monologue.

As you mature in terms of aging,
Does it ever get old?
Harboring hate and massaging malice,
Putting out venomous poison and vitriol

We can no longer take extended blinks,
And act like it's all games and fun when the,
Vertical blue men under sheets
Put black men under sheets, horizontally.

If you want to make America great again,
Take away the hate and then,
Maybe we will see that death is the pricey wage,
That is paid for sin.

Putting God back into places you took Him from,
Is something you should choose to explore.
They can find arms for the war,
But no alms for the poor on domestic soil.

The Fox is guarding the hen house,
When it is the crooks who decide the laws.
And evangelicals aren't spreading good news—
Instead, their greatest commission is their common cause.

Just Believe

The mind is such a marvelous machine;
It's profound in the things it can conceive.
But so much more could be achieved,
If we would only, first, choose to believe.

In those times I thought I wouldn't make it,
And could not withstand the hour.
He demonstrated that His grace is sufficient,
And allowed me a measure of His staying power.

I AM A MAN—nothing more, nothing less;
I won't lie and tell you I've been perfect.
But without any hesitation and no pause or reservation,
Because I believe, I know I'm worth it.

Palm readers MIGHT guess it right,
But you go to them, yet and still,
But you refuse to believe He can bring you through,
When He has cattle on a thousand hills.

If star signs tell you that you're crazy,
You will believe, undoubtedly, what they say,
But you hesitate to trust who hung the stars,
And knows them all by name.

Believing the creation with no faith in the creator,
Will only prove to be a rocky road.
That's like believing artificial intelligence,
But doubting the one who sat to write the code.

Our anxieties could calm,
And our depressing thoughts could be easily relieved,
If we chose to rest in the blanket of faith,
And make the simple choice to believe.

I would rather live believing,
And find, in death, that I was wrong,
Than to do the opposite,
And learn differently when I am dead and gone.

Enemy of Anonymity

The thing about anonymity,
Is it offers the protection of the crowd.
It heightens cries and emboldens jokers,
Who, otherwise, wouldn't dare to say it out loud.

It allows the use of intimidation,
And for cowards to peddle fear.
What internet trolls are doing, now,
Has been around and on the scene for many years.

In a group, they can be as loose as a goose,
But remain themselves on their own during the day.
If anyone needs an example of this,
Just look at the way of the KKK.

These clowns in white dunce caps,
Are not the only example to find.
Just look at the Sanhedrin as they stoned Stephen,
Way back in the biblical times.

Anonymity allows the loudest critic,
To remain a nameless and seemingly silent party.
You see and hear their slurs and sentiments,
But, then, they blend back into the body.

It's a strategy that is cowardly—
A method that makes mice of men so manly.
Timidity in place of resolve,
And, quite frankly, I cannot stand it.

If you need examples of how this happens,
Even today, in this present age,
Just look to the internet thugging,
That's done from behind the comfort of screen names.

Just turn to social media,
Or look at comments on any website,
And you will see the toughest talk,
From those who won't burst a grape in a fruit fight.

I, myself, am a man of peace,
But I say this with no regrets.
We all need to keep the same energy,
When it is time to stand by ourselves.

Likadosia

Without a doubt, social media has taken a toll on life—
An alternative reality in which we live.
Often, we give our all to get likes,
From folks who don't even fool with us, for real.

We post videos like they can't wait,
Opinions that, otherwise, we would never state.
And even give away our personal space,
When we post pics of the plates we ate.

Why and for what—
What do really get from it?
A measurable number of likes,
And the jackpot when we get them to comment?

I say the old days had it better;
Validation through social media, it wasn't.
The way they knew someone liked their perspective,
Was if they stood with them in public.

If they showed off pics of their kids,
It was the wallet insert giving the fuzzy wuzzies.
Not showing them to whoever may be looking and lurking online,
Standing pigeon toed with a peace sign and the duck lips.

I am a social media user, too;
This isn't any indictment of malice or spite.
Just saying we get lackadaisical on truly living life,
When it becomes just about the likes.

Game of Absolutes

As we grow and go through life,
We will see, if we look, that something is constant.
What can improve but we cannot outgrow,
Is what is commonly called our moral compass.

The moral compass will guide you,
Through any values that you may have.
And will stand to give you real-time alerts,
If you should drift from your chosen path.

Just like those that a scout might use,
To lead them in the right direction,
This one is relied upon for guidance,
When integrity is subject to testing.

But what is unique about this compass,
Is what causes it to pull and draw,
Is that it is rooted in what you have come to know,
As absolute right and wrong.

Low-Hanging Fruit

It's voluptuous and succulent,
Quite appealing to the eyes.
Coveted much and that is why,
As such, it should come as no surprise.

Smiles are formed from its viewing;
Aromas and juices often accompany laughter.
It's exterior is implicitly exquisite,
But it's the inward fruit that the world is after.

Getting to its counterparts,
Might require the assistance of a ladder.
While use of a stick can be used,
To exploit this low-hanging fruit all the better.

Vwap! Swat! Pow!,
Just one hit will knock it free.
Who cares about what's best for it;
The swinger only selfishly wants to see release.

What the lovers of the jelly,
May or may not know,
Is that the weight that the fruit carries,
Is what has it hanging so low.

Easy accessibility leaves it most unprotected and vulnerable,
Be it right or wrong.
It is the easiest to reach,
Because it's been hanging low for far too long.

Miranda Rights

They start with the right to remain silent,
And though this could prove to be true,
My primary concern in writing this
Is that anything you say can be used against you.

Go ahead and pour out your heart;
Tell your man what's on your mind.
Give him pearls and nuggets into you;
Just don't be surprised, how he uses the treasures he finds.

Please don't misunderstand me;
I'm not saying that you have something to hide.
I'm not advocating you to become a hermit,
Or keep it all bottled up inside.

What I will tell you, though,
Is not every smiling face is an angel.
Not everyone has your best interest at heart;
Not all that life throws at you can you handle.

So, please heed my warnings;
Maybe my experience will convince you
That you are free to speak as you wish,
But your own words may end up used against you.

Put Out

Better put some substance to it,
And not just be content with becoming a passing fashion.
Stop grandstanding to get attention,
If you're not willing to match talk with some action.

When offered to be relegated and reduced,
Insist against and flat out refuse.
Leaving the flesh on the shelf, so you can be, yourself, refreshed—
Put out to the world something that can be better used.

Let staying be your end game instead of parlaying;
I'm just saying.
Sometimes, the ones who say they're praying
Are the same ones who are really preying.

People say that they'll die with
All of the people that they ride with;
Just get down and out,
And see if they'll provide you enough eye water to cry with.

.

They stroll the mall, all day, with you—
For Saturday night, y'all make your plans.
Wanna really learn where you all stand?
See how she treats the wandering eye of your lustful man.

They put you out there to live life loosely,
And make your false self-image seem legit.
Behind your back, they say you're wrong for that,
And play you like nothing more than a cheap trick.

The gossip that they give to you
Helps to influence the way you think.
They gas you up to wear your clothes short and tight,
Using what God gave you to get free rounds of drinks

When guys jump at your cleavage and booty shorts,
Your friends tell you to 'YOLO,'
But when you choose to heed their advice,
They whisper and say you are just a hoe.

Sweetheart, curb that baggage and trash;
Strive to set your spirit free.
When they try to draw you into what's below your worth,
You better tell them, "Baaaby PLEASE!"

Because, just like a dog will take a bone,
If they love to bring one back,
They would let you fend alone,
If you ever separate from the pack.

Don't let your worth hinge on what you wear;
Don't feel you need validation from friends and,
Understand that what's priceless should be tended and hidden;
Your real value is what is intrinsic.

Don't allow yourself to be used to get dudes;
You are nobody's pawn to facilitate fun.
When you realize your only competition is your former self,
Then, baby girl, you have already won.

Pit Maneuver

I have observed something, many times on tv;
It's called "the pit maneuver," and is done by police.
From dramas and research, what I have been told,
The cop hits the other car from the back, and spins it out of control.

I have no dreams of policing, caught within my sight;
I just believe that, in some ways, it parallels to real life.
I saw it mostly in college, but not there, alone;
There were cases of it, before I even ever left my parents' home.

A guy would pursue a girl,
Wanting to get with her.
And in her suspecting nothing,
It would be in that, that she'd let him hit her.

Regardless of what she was pursuing,
Whether she was casual or busy.
When he finally hit her from the back,
He sent her life spinning into a tizzy.

It could be my imagination,
Or there could be some truth to it.
So it is all up to you,
What you choose to do with it.

I hope the wise take heed,
And the blind choose to take notice.
That, sometimes, when there's a simple hit,
It's just enough to make some of us lose focus.

Quid Pro Quo

No matter the endeavor,
Whether job, relationships or hustling.
Do not be fooled into thinking,
That you will ever get something for nothing.

I have lived thirty-four years,
And one thing has remained the same.
Any time something is received,
Something has to be exchanged.

To the layman, what "Quid Pro Quo" means,
Is more than just a philosophy.
It's the understanding that,
The world turns on reciprocity.

Trust it like you know it,
Because from birth date to this date,
I never met anybody
Who was giving anything away.

Sometimes, it may be like for like;
Other times, one party may be at a loss.
My Economics professor made it plain,
When he taught us that everything costs.

Trade Up

I've decided to lend some time
And give my honest evaluation
Of the mythical instant success that always comes
From getting an expensive college education.

I did it, so I feel qualified—
Like I have a place to state it.
For many of us, our choice was ingrained—
A product of the environment in which we were raised in.

We were a generation of promise,
Mostly birthed and raised of and by factory workers.
And they, themselves, were second-generation descendants,
Of sharecroppers who worked the earth and

Domestic workers who held positions of cooks and nannies;
They managed the households
Of well-to-do whites so that they might
Be able to help support their own families.

Wanting a life for their children and children's children
That didn't mean cooking with lard or weaving yarn,
They encouraged us to get an education,
So we wouldn't have to work as hard.

While I am grateful for their advice,
Given with the hopes that we would fulfill
Their hope for our better future,
I'd be remiss to not say that college degrees don't equal skills.

Don't mistake what I say—degrees have their place;
They tell potential employers you have the capacity to complete.
But, many times, that expensive paper
Doesn't equate to tangible money and food to eat.

Now that I have been and am back—
Because of my path, my plan has been laid.
I want to encourage those coming behind,
To consider the military and pursuing trades.

If I could rewind the hands of time,
Back to my senior year or so,
I would slow down and take about two years
And acquire a trade, so it could go where I go.

Then, enter college, so I could get knowledge
And be a participant in ROTC.
That way, I would exit, upon graduation,
As a commissioned officer—with my education free.

My Ol' Eyes

Change is a constant and,
Many times, comes, instantaneously;
If my sight and vision should ever have to leave,
I pray that they don't go, simultaneously.

It's my hope and so I stay in prayer
That I'll get to see what the end gon' be.
But know my eyes weren't made to last,
So I lay out, now, what my mind's eye sees.

I keep my nose to the grindstone
And try to leave no doubt or lack.
With preparation of unforeseen system or senses' failure,
While everything is still intact.

I don't know that I would trust someone
To write down what I might say.
No matter how much I would try to convey,
I'd doubt that they could say it my way.

So I put so much in your face,
While I have the faculty of all my senses.
And in black and white,
Is where I will constantly print this.

Burden, Me Not

If I should happen to get a bad report,
And my untimely demise becomes all but certain,
I want to face death as I have lived my life—
Wanting never to be someone else's burden.

If things do not go as I had hoped,
Or if my sight should become blurry about me,
Promise me you won't lend pity
And that you will not worry about me.

I'd like to think that I'll take it like old timers—
Trusting that my God will make a way for me.
It's not that I intend on quitting;
I'll just run on and see what the end gon' be.

See, I am confident that if I take sick,
Or if, to me, some sort of harm should come,
I will go to receive treasures I have stored up in Heaven,
And Jesus will welcome me home into His loving arms.

I have no plans of leaving anytime soon;
I just want to be sure that you know.
So I am telling you while my mind is sound,
Just in case the time comes and I have to go.

Don't you dare waste a minute worrying about me;
You had better not grieve the event of my demise.
I assure you that I won't, so you shouldn't;
I know exactly where my future lies.

Ease your mind; please and thank you;
I haven't received any disparaging news.
Just in case the unforeseen should happen,
I feel comfortable having told you what to do.

Do not have the medics to shock my chest;
If I should flat line, believe it was for the best.
I would have worked while it was light;
After sundown, please just allow me to rest.

Old Soul

I'd prefer you to laugh and reminisce—
I would hate for sadness or lack to make you cry.
Say that this old soul lived a full life;
Now, this old soul has taken to the sky.

Hunter Johnson Presents…

Dear Reader,

 Thank you for taking the time to join me for my eighth self-published work. Before I go on, I HAVE to give all glory to God. I know that I have said it, often, but never in a million years could I have imagined that I would be acknowledging the completion and publication of my EIGHTH BOOK! Jesus is a way maker! There are many who have just finished reading this who have been with me from the beginning, pushing me to reach higher and go harder—even when I felt like I had nothing left to give. For that, I am ever grateful. I cannot repay you for your support nor can I name everyone, individually; however, please know that this is our collective journey, and there would be no me as a writer without you as a reader.

 Since I was a child, I have been told, "You have an old soul" or have heard, "That boy's been here before." For a long time, I didn't give it much thought. After further examination, I realized that what people were trying to say is that, in some areas and toward some topics, I had a greater understanding—a deeper way of viewing things. I say what I have continuously said: as long as God gives it to me, I will give it to you. I sincerely hope that something within these pages has touched you in some way and will help to benefit your life. Be blessed and Godspeed.

-HJ

www.ingramcontent.com/pod-product-compliance
Lightning Source LLC
Chambersburg PA
CBHW051831090426
42736CB00011B/1754